Pinewood

Winning by the Rules

Phillip C. Reinke

Eloquent Books

Eloquent Books
An imprint of Strategic Book Group
P.O. Box 333
Durham CT 06422
www.StrategicBookGroup.com

ISBN: 978-1-60911-153-3

Printed in the United States of America

To My Dad...

...who taught me many valuable lessons...

...of them...

...the most important one was...

...how special the time was that we spent together...

To Lori...

...to the best...

. . . who gave the support . . .

. . . that made this and many other things happen . . .

To Grey Owl...

...although your voice came from the shadows...

...and I knew who you were...

...I listened and learned from you...

Contents

Introduction

"We want a short and concise guide... We do not need filler... We do not have time to read page after page to find out what not to do... Tell us what to do and how to do it...and we'll be happy." That is what I continuously received as feedback as I passed out photocopies of my guidebook to interested dads and Cub Scouts. When I sat down to finalize this guide, I had that single goal in mind, to make it as brief and valuable as it could be.

This guide to building faster pinewood derby racers, without breaking the rules, contains both a detailed description of our discoveries and a "Quick Guide" section that incorporates most of the characteristics of a winning racer. If time does not allow for detailed reading, jump to the final chapter of the book, and follow those guidelines.

Please remember that you are one of many racers competing for the same thing. Everyone is trying to build a winning racer.

Nothing guarantees victory, especially cheating! What is guaranteed is that by doing your best and being an honest and true competitor, with good sportsmanship, you'll have a great time and learn many things along the way.

Good luck, and may you build the fastest racer ever!

1

Winning by the Rules

THE PINNACLE CAR COMPANY

Pinnacle Car Racing (PCR) is a fictitious company, founded by my son (Tyler) and me. Although it's stated purpose was to build and race winning pinewood derby racers, its real purpose was to show an eight-year-old boy what his father did for a living. During the course of Pinnacle's three-year history, it created three pinewood derby racers that won three district championships. Winning a single district race is an accomplishment in and of itself, but a streak of three is a good indicator that PCR found a winning combination. Even more impressive was that each racer that PCR entered was progressively faster.

At the end of Tyler's racing career, and his retirement from Pinnacle's leadership, he suggested that we share what we learned about building pinewood racers in the form of a book. His reasoning was to give other Cub Scouts a chance to have as much fun with their dads as he did working with me! How could I turn that down? So before closing the doors of Pinnacle Car Racing forever, we wrote this book.

I am an industrial engineer, a Six Sigma Certified Master Blackbelt, working primarily on shifting organizations' cultures and methodologies into more customer-focused and profitable modes. Trying to explain what I do to support our family is more difficult than the job that I have. Rather than submitting Tyler to long-winded explanations that are way beyond his attention span, I made him president of a company that builds pinewood derby racers, and I performed the role that I do with the companies that I work for.

My job combines science, engineering, and statistics with other disciplines. For the sake of our work at PCR, we would focus on the engineering aspects of my job. That is just what we did while we designed, built, and tested his racers. There was one critical characteristic that the racers had to maintain while we did that. They had to conform to every rule of the race. Using statistical tools, we would hypothesize what effect a change would have on the performance of his racer and test for actual statistical significance. Those things that mattered to the speed and consistent performance of his racer were added to the design, and we continued to discover new things.

When the big races occurred, we made notes of how his racer actually performed and also made notes related to his competition, just like real companies should be doing! Over the course of time, we learned much and rejected even more!

As you can probably conclude, our hobby was not a two-weeks-before-the-race-type effort. PCR Research and Development operated year-round! But to conform to the race rules, every racer was constructed in the month prior to the Pack race, with the kit provided by the Pack. The only exception to this was Tyler's first racer. It was designed and built in the two weeks prior to the race. From that point onward, the designs for the new and improved racers began immediately after the last race.

This brings us to another reason for writing this book. When Tyler and I set out to build his first racer, we went to the Internet to capture as much background information as possible. What we found was *very* disheartening!

Not once did we find a single booklet about how to win by the rules. In fact, the Internet is loaded with information on how to cheat and get away with it, not to mention just as many dealers selling machined wheels, axles, lubricants, and bodies, all guaranteeing faster speeds (even though they are well beyond the limits of the rules). We also found places where one can purchase racers (already built) that supposedly won previous district championships! We purchased many of these items and tested them. Many we found made a difference, while others didn't. What we wanted to know was the capability of our competition, even if they cheated, and how to ensure that our performance exceeded theirs (within the rules).

As we were gathering information, Tyler asked if cheating in the pinewood derby broke the bigger Scout rules, "You know, Dad, like the ones about honesty?" My response was an emphatic, "Yes!"

Awareness of what was out in the market often allowed us to identify racers with machined axles or machined wheels. Tyler and his racer were rewarded for their honesty and integrity by victory, even over those who chose to try win by cheating. I recall a few sideline "Shhhhhs" when a young man would (somewhat loudly) say to his dad, "I thought you said those special axles would make us win."

Rather than filling a book with conjecture and theories, as many of the available books do, we will share only those aspects that we tested and showed actual statistical significance. There are also a few myths that we will note as making no difference. Over the course of four years, we hypothesized hundreds of characteristics and tested each. Many did not show any statistical difference, and a few made big differences. One would think that there are not enough things related to building a racer out of a block of wood, four nails, and four plastic wheels to write a book about! The very opposite is true; in fact, we are still discovering things, and you will too!

How big were the differences? During the second year of PCR's existence, and the weekend before the race, we received a call from a fellow Scout, who needed help building his racer. In one evening, we built and painted the racer, applying the design features that the time allowed us. That year, Tyler's racer took first place, and his friend's racer took second place. The only racer that beat his friend's racer was Tyler's! Those same techniques are described in the "Quick Guide" section.

2

What Is the Real Purpose of the Pinewood Derby?

The pinewood derby is more than fifty years old! There are many lessons and experiences that young Scouts have learned from participating in it. Although this is not a complete list, some are:

- Basic woodworking skills
- The ability to design and create what he visualizes
- The ability to dream
- Sportsmanship
- Competition
- Painting
- Creativity
- Structure
- Patience
- Honesty
- Fair play

The most important lesson for a Scout to learn is to do his best! Competition brings out the best and worst in people. I have seen many fathers and sons push the limits and actually break the rules in order to win. As previously noted, many of the racers that Tyler's racers competed against and beat were built with non-stock wheels and axles. What was important to us and Tyler's company was that his racers won by the rules. PCR did not want any victory to be hollow. "Doing your best" to Tyler and PCR meant learning and applying everything we possibly could to pinewood derby racers. If we lost after that, we were still proud to have done our best.

The combination of the existence of cheaters and Tyler's reputation as a winning racer created a situation where he and his cars went under ever-increasing scrutiny. At first, this was very upsetting to Tyler, and he had a hard time understanding why people would think that he would cheat, especially after the painstaking measures we took to ensure that we complied with the rules.

There was one individual at the district level who tried every year to take away much of the joy from Tyler. One year he stood behind us and continually complained about "that black racer" being "the furthest thing from legal as he had ever seen." The next year, to our surprise, he was an inspector. He took advantage of his position and made Tyler remove his wheels and axles to prove that they were stock. Although we could blame his cynical behavior toward Tyler and his racers on cheaters, this man had no place in Scouting and was ruining more boys than he helped. Yet I learned an important lesson from Tyler when he said, "I don't pay much attention to him, Dad. He is just jealous of the fact that I have a dad who works with me on my racer! Let's make sure that we mention him in our book! Perhaps it will help him feel bad about how he hurts the boys, and he'll be nicer to them." Then Tyler suggested that we name the book *Winning by the Rules*. "This will help that old man understand what we did."…I wholeheartedly agreed!

3

My First Pinewood Derby

Although it is more than thirty-five years ago, one of my fondest childhood memories is building a pinewood derby racer with my father. I vividly recall every moment from the day I received the kit at a Pack meeting, through the dreaming and designing, the smell of the wood, the first cut, the endless shaping and sanding, the painting, and finally the races!

My father worked rotating shifts, and during the construction, it was one of the very few times that I was allowed to wait up for him to get home (at 11:00 P.M.) so that we could work for a few precious moments on my racer! How I cherished those fleeting moments! My father was never satisfied with anything less than giving our best effort. My racer was a symbol of that ethic.

The Pack race was set up in a gymnasium at our local elementary school. I was very excited. Although my father was working, he was there right beside me in this race, and I stood proudly in the registration line with the product of *our* work clutched tightly in my hands.

At the Pack-level race, my racer was given an award for best design and paint job. If this was the only recognition that I received, I was a proud and happy Scout! It was my first opportunity to be the best of about 125 other boys!

The race was just as eventful. My racer placed first in the Pack! It went undefeated and beat a classmate by more than a racer length! I, again, was very proud and even more proud that my friend and I would together represent our Pack at the district race.

About one month later, we arrived at a local community hall for the district race. It was very different from our Pack race. In the center of the hall was the track. This area was militaristically controlled. Outside of the roped area, the crowd churned with excitement. Our district was very active. The district race had more than one hundred boys competing. I registered my racer and found a place to sit and wait for my car to race.

As I sat, I spotted my friend seated directly across from me. He spotted me too! I had an open seat next to me, and I motioned him to join me, which he did. I told him that I was here alone because my father had to work. I then asked him where his father was, and he told me that his father was helping with the race.

We sat and watched race after race until it was finally time for our racers to run down the ramp. That is when I noticed that my friend's father was the guy who carried the racers from their parking places and placed them on the track for the race. My friend's racer ran in the first heat and won. My racer ran in the third heat and won. My friend and I cheered each other's racers on to victory. Then the inevitable happened; the final race was announced, and it was between the two of us!

As my friend's dad carried the two racers to the track, he accidentally dropped my racer, and a wheel popped off! I was crushed and ran through the crowd to see if I could repair it. Despite the best efforts of a few *very* helpful and supportive fathers, it could not be made as good as new, and my racer went on to take second place.

4

The Pinewood Derby Rules

The first thing that you have to know when entering the pinewood derby is the *exact* rules. These are the determining factors in what you can and can't do. They often vary from Pack to Pack and district to district. In our experience, spanning three different districts and several Internet searches, the differences were not significant.

THE DERBY CONSTRUCTION RULES

- The racer must be constructed with the components in the kit provided by the Pack.
- A majority of the work must be done by the Cub Scout.
- The wheels and axles must be officially authorized Cub Scout components.
- Only graphite or the official Cub Scout Teflon lubricant can be used to lubricate the wheels and axles.

- The racer cannot exceed seven inches long.
- The racer's width cannot exceed two and three-quarter inches.
- The axles must be visible in the wheel slots.
- The racer's weight cannot exceed five ounces.
- The racer must run by gravity only.
- The racer must have a track clearance of three-eighths inches.
- All decorative parts must be securely fastened to the racer.
- If lead is used to weight the racer, it must be sealed in the body or painted in such a way to minimize exposure.

The following is an example of race rules used by Cub Scout Pack 266 in Ponte Vedra Beach, Florida. This Pack runs a fantastic derby. Their rules were created with the intent that if a Scout conformed and then competed in other races, there would be a high probability that the racer would conform to the host's rules. Before beginning construction of your racer, gather the specific requirements for your Pack and district. This will save the disappointment of not being able to race.

PINEWOOD DERBY RULES

Pack Derby Announcement, Rules and Guidelines

The pinewood derby is open to all active Cub Scouts in Pack 266.

Racers should be built by the Cub Scout with adult guidance. The amount of adult guidance and help will vary somewhat with the age and experience of the Scout. Keep in mind the purpose of the project/race is to support family values and learning.

The Pack 266 pinewood derby will take place Thursday and Friday, January 27–28.

Thursday, January 27, is the inspection and weigh-in for the racers at Rawlings Elementary School, in the cafeteria. Racers must be presented to the Pack racing committee Thursday, January 27, between 7:00 and 8:30 P.M. The Pack racing committee will inspect and weigh the racers to ensure compliance with the general rules for all races. The details of the inspection are outlined below. After a racer has been inspected and accepted, the racer will remain with the Pack racing committee until completion of the race the following night. Inspection takes only a few minutes, and parents and Scouts are free to go as soon as the racer is accepted. Only racers meeting the requirements before the close of the inspection will compete in the race.

Friday, January 28, is the race at the Rawlings Elementary School in the gymnasium.

Races will be run by rank/age of the Scouts. Each rank should take about thirty minutes to run. The approximate racing schedule is:

Tigers: 6:30 P.M.
Wolves: 7:00 P.M.
Bears: 7:30 P.M.
Webelos I: 8:00 P.M.
Webelos II: 8:30 P.M.
Pack Run-off Finals: 9:00 P.M.

Scouts will race against the other Scouts in their rank. First, second, and third places will be determined for each rank. The first-, second-, and third-place finishers for each rank can advance to the district races. The fourth-place finisher will be the alternate if one of the racers cannot race at the district level.

Each Scout will race against all other Scouts in his rank. For example, if there are eight Tiger Scouts racing, each Tiger Scout will race seven times, once against each of the other seven Tigers. The winner of each race will receive two points, and the second-place finisher will receive one point. Within each rank, the Scout with the highest number of points will be first place; the Scout with the next highest number of points will be second place, etc. If Scouts are tied with the same number of points, there will be a race-off to break the tie.

Once all ranks have raced, the first-, second-, and third-place finishers from each of the five ranks will run in a double-elimination race-off to determine the first-, second-, and third-place racers for the Pack.

Racers incurring damage may be repaired, as long as the repair time does not exceed five minutes. If the racer cannot be repaired within the allotted time, all subsequent races for that racer will be counted as losses, and race placement/position will be calculated as such.

Unsportsmanlike conduct by any entrant or member of the audience will be grounds for expulsion from the competition and/or race area.

GENERAL RULES FOR ALL RACES

Entrant must use the parts from the official Grand Prix Pinewood Derby Kit No. 1622. Racers must be built in the current year (since last year's pinewood races) and not previously raced.

1. Vehicle Dimensions and Weight

   a. Width: not to exceed two and three-quarter inches.

   b. Length: not to exceed seven inches.

   c. Weight: not to exceed five ounces or 141.75 grams.

   d. Ground clearance: there must be sufficient clearance (approximately three-eighths of an inch) between the bottom of the racer body and the track.

2. Assembly and Accessories

   Racer modifications must not exceed the dimension and weight limits!

   a. Washers, bushings, and springs are prohibited.

   b. Specialty wheels and axles are prohibited (see 4 below).

   c. Racers must be freewheeling with *no* starting devices.

   d. Details, such as steering wheel and driver, are permissible as long as these details do not exceed the maximum length, height, and weight specifications.

   e. All parts and weights must be securely fastened to the racer.

   f. The racer body may be cut down and hollowed out, providing the wheels fit over the track guide strips, which are one and three-quarters inches wide.

   g. The racer body may be beefed up to increase weight. Wood, wood filler, putty, or metal may be used, provided the materials are securely affixed to the racer body.

   h. Racer bodies may be sanded, painted, and detailed.

3. Wheels and Axles

   a. Racer wheels must be those from the official Grand Prix Pinewood Derby Kit or official Grand Prix replacement wheels. Wheels may be sanded or polished smooth to remove seams, defects, and rough edges. V-shaped, double-V, or H-shaped wheels are not allowed. The wheels may not be cut down or narrowed.

b. Racer axles must be those from the Official Grand Prix Pinewood Derby Kit or official Grand Prix replacement axles. The axles may be polished. Axles may be lubricated with dry-powered lubricant (graphite). Silicone, liquid, or similar sprays and oils are prohibited and may damage plastic wheels.

4. Wheel Base

a. The wheel base (distance between the front and rear axle slots) may not be modified. Entrants must use the pre-cut axle slots so that the distance between the axles is the same for all racers. The axle slots must be visible on the bottom of the racer.

INSPECTION AND REGISTRATION OF RACERS

Each racer must be registered by the Scout who built the racer, and each racer must pass inspection by the Pack racing committee prior to racing. All racers will be inspected to ensure compliance with the General Rules for All Races listed above. If, at registration, a racer does not pass inspection, the owner will be informed of the reason the racer did not pass and will be given the opportunity to make adjustments to the racer. The Scout may adjust or alter his racer to bring his racer into compliance, provided, however, that all adjustments must be completed prior to close of the weigh-in. Upon passing inspection, the racer will be turned over to the Pack racing committee officials. Racers will remain with the Pack race officials until conclusion of the competition for that racer. The inspection committee has the right to disqualify racers that do not meet the criteria outlined in the race rules.

Every effort has been made to ensure that the race rules of Pack 266 are the same as the advanced competition levels. However, the fact that a racer has passed inspection from the Pack does not guarantee that it will pass for the district or council competition.

Following is a diagram that spells out the minimum and maximum dimensional requirements for a pinewood derby pacer. (See Figure 1.)

These are the requirements that must be followed in order to just get into the race. From this point forward, we will address those characteristics that make a winning racer.

Figure 1

5

The Laws Governing the Race

In the previous chapter, we reviewed a set of the rules for the race. These rules were created by people to set a level playing field for everybody. These rules can and often do change. But there are some laws of nature that cannot be changed. To fully understand how to build a winning racer, we need to know what these laws are and how they affect the race. Before we get into these laws, let's look at the race itself.

A race is a process! In its simplest form, a process is something that takes input(s), adds something to those input(s) through a series of steps, adds something to the input(s) as a result of the steps, and produces an output. As strange as it may sound (we need to say this again), a race is a process. It has inputs (the car and the ramp), and it has an output, which is the time that it takes the car to travel from the beginning of the ramp to the finish line. The steps of the process are as follows:

1. Add car to track by placing it against the starting pin.

2. Add gravity by releasing starting pin. As a result of gravity, the car achieves its maximum speed. The combination of speed and weight produces momentum.

3. When the car enters the horizontal portion of the track, the momentum (speed × weight) allows it to travel across the finish line, that is, if the momentum that it accumulates is sufficient to allow it to travel to the finish line.

4. After is crosses the finish line, any residual momentum stored in the car is expended by the stop at the end of the track.

That is the long and the short of the race. As simple as it sounds, there are quite a few unique forces at play. Understanding the effects of each of the forces is critical to identifying and optimizing the vital few and building a winning car.

Before you begin a scientific investigation and test theories, you need to fully understand the principals behind the process. You need to know what rules really come into play during the course of the process. For a pinewood derby racing car, you do not need to know the ugly details of Einstein's laws of relativity, but you do have to have an understanding of two of the three classical laws of Sir Isaac Newton! Of his three laws of motion, the first two are of most importance...but in reverse order. They are:

Law #2: Force (F) is proportional to mass (m) times acceleration (a) when proper units are chosen (F = ma).

Law #1: In the absence of net external force, a body either is at rest or moves in a straight line with constant velocity.

Actually we are going to add one other discovery from Galileo (two more principles), but we'll talk about that when it makes the most sense. By clearly defining the process of racing and the physical laws that affect the process, we can begin to convert our information into insight.

Let's put the process into a picture. (See Figure 2.)

THE RACE PROCESS

We can put some math behind our picture also!

The important part of the race is B + C.

The total race is B + C + D.

We can substitute numbers for the letters. The important numbers to us are:

- The amount of time it takes to travel each one of the distances specified by a letter.
- The average speed of the car for each letter-specified distance.
- The distance traveled for each letter-specified leg of the race.

The other important value that we will discuss is "F," or how fast the car is traveling. When you think about the complete race it is:

- How fast can you get from a dead stop (E) to the maximum speed (F)?
- How much of that speed can be retained across the length of (C)?
- How much energy must be expended to stop the car after the finish line?

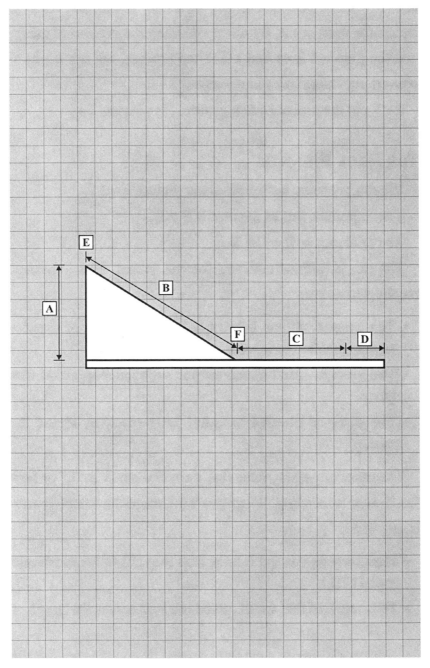

Figure 2

GETTING DOWN TO BUSINESS

Now that we know the laws of physics that are governing the race, it is important to understand how theses laws help or hinder. Earlier in this chapter, it was mentioned that there was one other law, actually a *principle,* governing the race... And that principle has been attributed, by some, to a man named Galileo.

Have you ever watched a pinewood derby race? If you have, you probably noticed that all of the cars were about even at the end of the slope. As the cars traveled along the flat part of the race, the differences widened... And by the finish line, there was a clear winner.

Before Galileo, people thought that weight made a difference to the speed at which an object fell. This actually goes back to a guy named Aristotle. What people believed was that an object weighing ten pounds dropped five times faster than an object weighing two pounds. According to legend, Galileo dropped two balls of different weights from the Tower of Pisa, and they hit the ground at the same time! He went on to create a formula for it. It is called the acceleration constant. We do not have to know how to do this, just that it exists.

Some people still believe that lighter or heavier cars are faster on the ramp (they are kind of right but for the wrong reasons). But if we were to take a three-ounce car and a five-ounce car up to the top of the Tower of Pisa and drop them, they would smash to bits at exactly the same time and at the same speed! If we did it over and over, it would always be the same. Laws of nature are like that!

PINEWOOD DERBY TERMINAL VELOCITY

Cars of different weights will go the same speed on the ramp because gravity attracts all objects the same way! The maximum effect that gravity can have on all of the cars is the same. We'll show that weight combined with gravity is the fuel of the car. If we were just racing to the end of the slope, the weight wouldn't matter. It does later when the real race begins!

To understand this, let's figure out how fast the car can be moving. We represent this by the letter/distance "A" in our drawing. There is a fancy calculation for determining the speed of an object falling at any given point (this is what Galileo figured out). And we could do that, but there is an easier way! Simply drop a ball from the same height as the ramp and time it. You'll find that it takes just less than a second to fall that distance. When the calculation (mentioned earlier) is applied, we see that the object hits the ground at about twelve miles per hour. That speed and time varies depending on how far you drop the ball.

I have had many discussions with engineers and physicists on the next piece of this scientific puzzle. Some said that the maximum speed should be calculated by the distance of the fall (A), and others said that it should be by the distance traveled (B). We picked the first alternative because it allowed us to use the other laws to optimize our car.

What we know for sure is that the speed of the car is determined by gravity. A two-ounce car and a five-ounce car will theoretically go the same speed. The speed is limited by the vertical distance or height of the ramp (that is what Galileo showed us). When we dropped and timed the ball, we created a performance standard. In theory, the car should go from the start (at the top of the ramp) to end of the ramp in less than a second (Galileo showed us how to calculate that). Most cars travel this distance on a standard length track in a little over one and a half seconds. Why? Newton's first law!

THE LAW THAT SLOWS THE CAR ON THE RAMP

Instead of quoting Newton's first law again (in a way that no one understands it), we'll put it into terms that makes sense to us!

If something is stopped, it will stay stopped unless something acts upon it; if something is moving, it will stay moving unless something acts upon it.

If the car was falling with nothing acting upon it (slowing it down), its speed would be exactly the same as that of the ball we dropped. However, it has a bunch of things acting on it, so it is slower. Most of what is affecting it is the ramp. If the ramp wasn't there when the car was released, it would fall at the same speed as the ball! But because it is there, it falls, but not as fast.

Why?

The answer is simple when you know Newton's first law. Part of the gravity that is pulling down on the car (speeding it up) is being converted to friction on the track.

There are other forces at work on the car at this point. They are more about engineering than science, so we'll discuss them later in the book. What we know for sure is that the speed of the car is determined by the following calculation:

Car Speed = Galileo's Constant—Newton's First Law

Kind of funny! Since we cannot go any faster than what Galileo told us we can, we will focus our efforts around minimizing the impact of Newton's first law. That is enough discussion on this part of the race. Let's move on to where the real race takes place!

THE REAL RACE

What we discovered is that, all things being equal, a two-ounce car and a five-ounce car will be going the same speed at the end of the slope. Why do they cross the finish line at different speeds? That answer comes to us with an understanding of Newton's second law combined with his first law!

We know that something moving will continue to move as long as it isn't acted upon by something else (like friction created by the downward force of gravity on the ramp). So theoretically, the cars should travel at the same speed forever...but they don't! Friction coming at the car from many different angles causes it to slow. Coming to the rescue is Newton's second law and the reason behind the differences in the finishes of the two cars.

Let's put this law into words that we can understand and apply to our race! If Galileo dropped a bowling ball and a marble from that tower, I would prefer to get hit by the marble! We know that both will be traveling at the same speed, and both will hurt, but there is another force that is important. It is called momentum!

Although objects fall at the same speed, they have different momentums. We know that the heavier an object is, the more its momentum. When we put momentum in the context of the race, it is like the fuel of the car. It can be described as how much fuel or how good the fuel is; it doesn't matter. What matters is that the car needs to get as much fuel as possible while it is on the ramp. This is why weight is important. We know that the heavier the object, the more momentum it will amass during a given distance fallen. So the first thing that we know is that we need to make the car as heavy as allowed (five ounces is the usual upper limit). The other thing we know is that the farther the object falls, the faster it will go. So what we want to do is put the weight in the back of the car, so that it falls the longest possible time!

After the car crosses the finish line and travels the remaining length of the track (D), there is some momentum left. This will become important to us when we are designing our car. We do not want to forget that!

Now that we have amassed the most amount of momentum, the race is about keeping it going with the minimal amount of influence from outside sources, such as friction. We have spent enough time in the theoretical world; it is now time for us to get to work.

6

Basic Tools and Support Materials

"Be prepared!" Where have we heard that before? Having the tools and equipment available is important. Our racers were built entirely with hand tools, with one exception, an electric drill. Here is a list of the items we used during the construction:

- Pinewood Derby Grand Prix Kit #1622
- Poster board or light cardboard (similar to the kind found in cereal boxes)
- #2 pencil
- Coping saw
- Rasp
- Drill bits
- Assorted sand paper (60, 120, 240 grit)
- Steel wool
- Graphite powdered lubricant
- Primer

- Paint
- Metal file
- Toothpicks
- Electric or hand drill
- Wood putty/filler (to correct mistakes)

You should also have access to a scale that allows you to weigh your racer in grams or tenths of an ounce. A postal scale works well.

Some other or optional tools and equipment that help are:

- A Cub Scout Wheel Tuning Kit, available at your local Scout or hobby store. It has a wheel arbor for ensuring the wheels are round, extra axles, and polishing grit.
- A Cub Scout Wheel Alignment Tool, available at your local Scout or hobby store. It has all of the clearances laid out along with cutouts to help ensure the wheels are tracking straight.
- Racer weights. There are many different types available. Your Scout or hobby store also supplies them.
- An extra set of wheels, available at you local Scout or hobby store.

7

Things That Don't Matter

The best way to start designing and building your racer is to know what not to do or what to avoid. Then by combining that knowledge with those design characteristics that you want to include, the racer seems to design itself, and as you will see, the possibilities are still endless!

During our testing, we found that there were quite a few things that we wholeheartedly believed would make a difference in the speed of the racer. These are things that most people would have bet big on! The results indicated that it made no difference, and sometimes, they actually detracted from the speed!

Special wheels and axles are not necessarily faster.

We found that machined wheels and axles did make a difference in the speed of the racer. However, the difference was not enough that good workmanship and creative thought could not do better! The temptation is always there to use things to give you an edge. Don't fall prey to the temptation.

Aerodynamic racers are not faster.

Actually the first series of tests that we ran were all focused on finding the best aerodynamic shape. What we discovered is that an aerodynamic shape has no effect on the speed of the racer. A little deeper analysis explained why. Although the racer appeared to be flying down the track, the fastest speed that we ever clocked over the course of the forty feet was just over twelve miles per hour. At this rate of speed, wind resistance does not measurably impact the speed.

It is important to note that aerodynamics should not be confused with body shape. Body shape (as you will later see) does play an important part. Our first racer used a combination of aerodynamics and, by chance, some other body design characteristics. We were misled by the design characteristics into believing that aerodynamics played an important role. (We later tested our given assumption and confirmed that the speed of a simple wheeled block was not significantly different from a wedge shape!)

Special lubricants do not increase speed.

We tested various lubricants and found that there was no significant difference. Nothing beat plain old graphite.

A perfect paint job does not increase the speed of a racer.

Paint has no statistically significant impact on the speed of the racer. Some would contend that a slick air stream is important, but this is directly related to aerodynamics. It is not significant. However, a sloppy paint job can hurt a racer's performance. Do not get paint on the axles or wheels. A good-looking racer can be a matter of pride. Tyler primed, painted, and repainted as many as sixteen times on a single racer to get the perfect, glass finish that he wanted. Although he knew that the finish really didn't matter, doing anything less than that would not have been doing his best.

Now that we know what doesn't really matter, let's move on…

8

Things That Matter

To understand how to design winning racers, we set about getting a full understanding of the factors that influence a racer's speed. We found that those design elements that made positive, statistical differences in the speed of the racer can be generalized into two categories, weight optimization and friction reduction. If you think about the racer in its most simplistic form, there are two forces in play during its trip down the ramp. The first force is working to speed it up (gravity) and the second force (drag in the form of friction) is slowing it down.

9

Racer Strength

As funny as it may sound, a racer needs to be built to race. Crash strength is important. If the racer is built properly, crashes during the race itself are rare, if nonexistent. However, we learned an important lesson, not through experimenting, but by direct experience.

In a tri-state gathering of various districts at a jamboree-type event, we were racing as representatives of our district. In all of the previous races, the racers were stopped at the end of the race by having them fall into a soft cushion or by their driving under a cloth. In this race, a foam block was set directly in the racers' paths. The racers ran down the track, crossed the finish line, and crashed into the block. Tyler's racer (The Black Manta) was designed and built with speed in mind and absolutely no regard to strength. In the first three races, Tyler's racer finished first and had the fastest overall speed (lowest average time). On the fourth race, tragedy struck. His racer crashed into the foam wall (as it had in three previous races), and a wheel broke off. Although we had sufficient time to repair the break, the racer did not run as well and actually dropped out of the race.

The first thing that we designed into every racer, from that point forward, was crash strength. Prior to painting the racer, we saturate it in wood harder to ensure overall strength.

10

Gravity and Weight

Five-ounce racers are faster.

We asked ourselves, "What powers the racer?" The answer is simple. Gravity! Gravity is both the engine and the fuel of the racer. When the racer is standing still at the starting gate, gravity is the fuel. We tested various weights and found that the maximum weight (five ounces, by the rules) is statistically the best. In other words, you want your racer to have a full tank of fuel!

As soon as the racer begins moving, gravity becomes the engine of the racer. The second characteristic that we found and tested simply confirmed a basic physics theorem. The weight needs to fall as long as possible to convey the maximum amount of energy to the racer. In other words, the weight needs to be as far back on the racer as possible. The *best* racer is a "rear engine" racer.

Racer design gets a bit more complicated when you take the next two characteristics into account. These two characteristics make a significant difference in minimizing the variation from race to race.

In some racing events, the overall winner is determined by best average speed over the span of a certain number of races. Therefore, it's important not only to be fast, but also being consistent is critical. We determined that weight distribution plays an important role in minimizing the overall variation. In a theoretical sense, the fastest racer would be the one with all five ounces of its weight as far back as possible. However, the configuration of the track adds another challenge to our design. The racer's path is controlled by its wheels straddling a raised area (guide). If the racer is poorly weighted, or its wheel alignment is bad (as we'll address in a later section of our book), it will wobble as it races down the track. This wobbling causes the racer's wheels to rub against the track. The rubbing causes friction, which in turn slows the racer down. The more the wheels rub, the slower the racer speed.

The opposite is also true; the straighter the racer travels down the track, the faster and more consistent its speed. When we began testing various design characteristics, we found that weight distribution was very important. Although we found that minimizing the amount of weight on the front wheels provided the fastest speeds, even minor variations in the track's surface caused the front wheels to hop! The result of this hop is even more disastrous, in that the racer often leaves its lane and crashes. Therefore, we optimized the distribution and found that an eighty/twenty distribution worked the best.

Racers with an eighty/twenty weight distribution are faster.

We found that 20 percent of the weight, or one ounce, should be on the front wheels of the racer, and 80 percent, or four ounces, of the total racer's weight should be on the rear wheels.

To check this, we simply built a small platform that was exactly the same height as the top of our scale. You don't have to be as fancy! Stacking a few books next to the scale has exactly the same effect; just make sure that the scale bed and the platform are the same height. Next, set the racer so that the rear wheels are on the platform and the front wheels are on the scale. The scale should read one ounce (or very near to that amount). Turn the racer around, placing the front wheels on the platform and the rear wheel on the scale. The weight should be very close to four ounces. This weight distribution becomes even more critical as we add more design elements. (See Figure 3.)

In actuality, this leads us to the shape of the racer! We have to design it with more wood in the back than in the front, therefore it becomes somewhat wedge shaped.

RACER WEIGHTING RECAP

- The racer should weigh as close to five ounces as possible without going over that amount.
- Eighty percent of the racer's weight should be as far back on the racer as possible.
- Twenty percent of the racer's overall weight should be on the front wheels.
- The weight should be placed as much as possible so that it runs directly down the centerline of the racer.
- The racer should be somewhat wedge shaped, allowing for an eighty/twenty weight distribution.

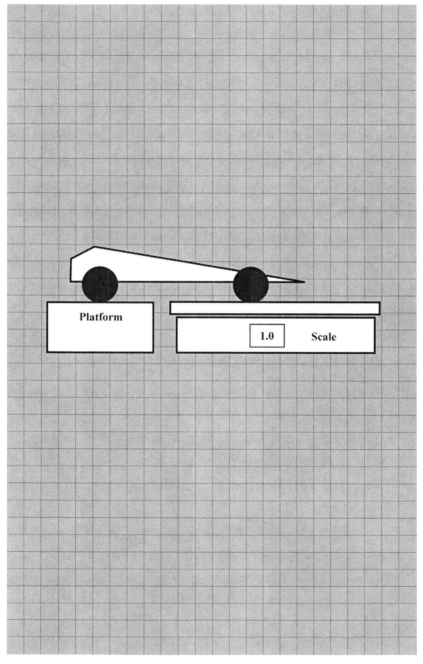

Figure 3

11

Friction

Even though we found that aerodynamics did not play a role in the speed of the racer, body design did. All of these design elements worked together to minimize the amount of friction that the racer encountered during its race.

We found that ground clearance played a significant role in speed. In fact, one of the rules specifies a minimum clearance of three-eighths inches. We found that removing as much wood from the bottom of the racer as possible, while allowing for sturdy and correct axle placement, provided the statistically best speeds. We also found that tapering the front end of the racer (its nose) improved speeds in some cases. Although some have contended that "the higher the nose, the sooner the start," we found no statistical differences. The upward tapered nose can make a difference when the racer moves from the ramp to the horizontal section of the run. If the racer's nose scrapes the track, it slows down. We have only encountered this on one track, but it pays to add this design element into your overall plan. I realize that this is hard to visualize, so all of these recommendations are included in the diagram at the end of this section.

While we are on the subject of the nose, let's exhaust all of the critical design elements related to it. One of the best ways to ensure that you are going to win races is to have a racer that runs down the track as straight as possible. If the racer starts straight and travels straight, the odds of winning are shifted in your favor.

Aligned racers are faster.

The best way to minimize variation in a process (and we consider a race a single run of a process) is to start the racer straight in the first place and have it travel straight down the track. The people who run the race are far too busy to ensure that every car is placed perfectly straight. At many pinewood derbies, literally a hundred races are run. To do that in a reasonable amount of time, the starter places the racers at the top of the track, with their noses against a starting pin. If the racer is not placed perfectly centered on the pin (or pointed to the left or right) as it is released, one of its front wheels will rub against the ridge until the racer aligns itself. This rubbing causes friction and results the racer losing speed that it will never regain.

To minimize the probability of misalignment, simply make the nose as narrow as possible. A narrow nose gives the starter a smaller area to work with. Another design feature to add to the racer, which promotes better alignment, is to make the front of the racer slightly concave, with the lowest point at the very center of the racer.

These two design features help ensure that the racer starts its race in good alignment.

If you were to draw these recommendations on your block, they would look something like the following figure. (See Figure 4.)

FRICTION RECAP

- Adequate ground clearance is critical. Design your racer to exceed the minimum three-eighths-inch clearance requirement

- Starting straight from the beginning of the race helps maximize overall speed. Narrow the nose of the racer to ensure that the racer starts straight.

- Consider painting a narrow strip down the center of the car (racing stripe). It will subtly help the guy placing the car on the track to align it.

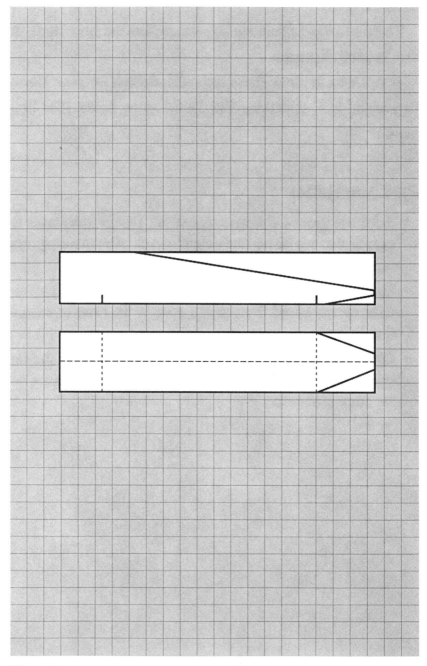

Figure 4

12

Body Design

Racers having minimal contact between the wheel hub and the racer's body are faster.

One of the most significant findings during our testing was the impact that the friction of the wheel hub against the body of the racer had on its speed. It is simultaneously important to hold the wheels one and three-quarter inches apart. To minimize the friction point, we tested many different configurations and found that the best solution was to remove as much wood from the area around the wheel hub as possible. (See Figure 5). Tyler relieved the friction point on his first two racers with simple hand tools. He and I drew lines on the blocks of wood, and he filed and sanded the wood out. When Tyler was able to use my router table, we sped the construction process up by simply running the block lengthwise across a beveled bit. In either case, it is important to have the hub hitting the smallest section of the body as possible.

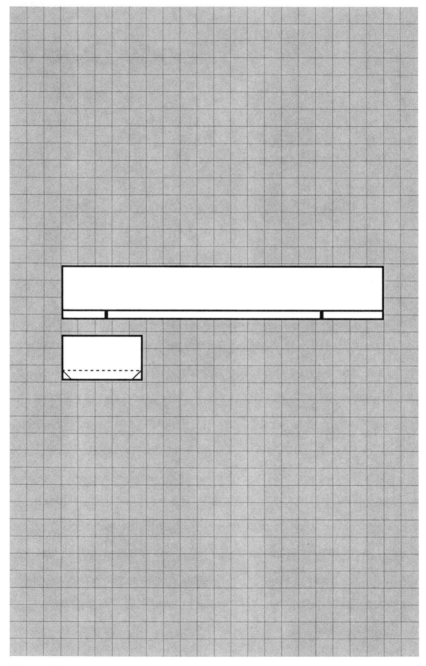

Figure 5

Designing the racer's body, with allowances for weighting, is important. In every racer, Tyler and I drilled holes where we wanted the weights located. We then melted fishing sinkers with a propane torch and poured the molten metal into the holes. If you choose to use this technique to weight your racer, please be very careful, and do this task in a *very* well ventilated area. Many sinkers still contain some amount of lead. The vapors emitted by the molten material can be very toxic. There are other ways to add weight to your racer. These vary from purchasing the precast weight from a local Scout or hobby shop and attaching it with screws or nails to gluing coins on the appropriate spots. (See Figure 6.)

In this drawing, you note that there are three holes. One hole is behind the rear axle, one hole is over the rear axle, and one is in front of the rear axle. The order in which weight is added to the racer goes as follows:

1. Add weight to the rear hole until no more can be added.
2. Add weight to the hole in front of the axle to counterbalance the rear weight. (See section on weight.)
3. Add final weight to the hole over the axle. This has no effect on the balance of the racer.

BODY DESIGN RECAP

Whatever method of weighting you choose, remember to follow these guidelines:

- The total racer weight should be as close to five ounces as possible without going over.

PHILLIP C. REINKE

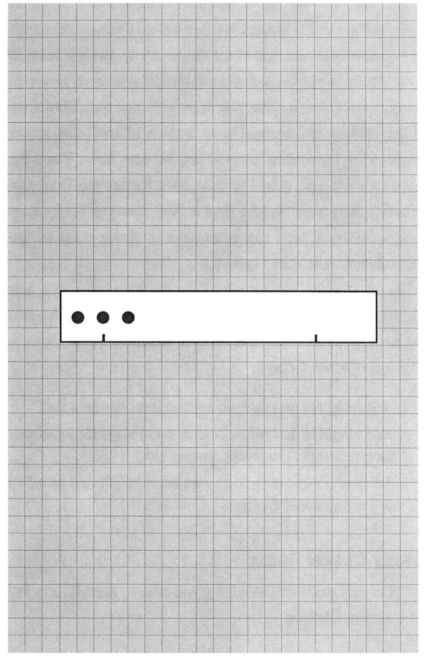

Figure 6

- Weight distribution should be as close to 80 percent rear and 20 percent front as possible. Using the previously mentioned technique, the weight at the rear wheels should be about four ounces, and the front should weigh about one ounce.

- A great design feature is to create a fine-tuning hole. Drill a small hole somewhere in the rear of the racer, in which you can add or subtract small pieces of weights to bring the racer to exactly five ounces, as measured by the official scale at the time of weigh-in.

- If you are using the precast weights, attach them to the top of the racer. Attaching them to the bottom increases the chance that the racer will bottom out and ultimately slow the racer down.

- Taper the area around the wheel slot to minimize the friction between the wheel hub and the body.

13

Wheels

The next two sections of this book address the most signifi-cant aspects of a winning racer, wheels and axles. We will begin on the outside of the drive train and work inward. The wheels that come with the kit are full of variation. Some of the wheels provided are not perfectly round, some have bits of plastic left from the molding process, and the list of defects can go on and on.

Round wheels are faster.

We found a very helpful and simple tool at the Scout shop called a "wheel arbor." This arbor is part of a wheel tune-up kit. It fits through the hub of the wheel and allows it to be turned by a drill. By turning the wheel in the drill and slightly sanding or filing the wheel, it can be brought to round, and the surface defects can be removed.

Clean hubs are faster.

Another finding is that wheel speed is more than skin deep! We found that some wheels ran faster than others. As we inspected them, we found some imperfections in the wheel hub itself. These imperfections may be from the molding process or could have been inadvertently made during the rounding process. Whatever the source of variation, we found that placing an axle/wheel assembly in a drill, and turning the axle in the direction opposite the direction that the wheel will turn as it travels down the track, makes a significant difference in racer speed. If you want to go the extra step further, make a thick paste with the pumice (polishing powder), which is included in the wheel tune-up kit, and put a small amount inside of the wheel hub before turning it. The same results can be achieved with a paste made with baking soda. After completing the internal tuning, be sure to thoroughly clean the wheels. These abrasive compounds can slow the racer slightly. Another caution is not to turn the inside of the hub too much. The plastic is a soft material. Turning the hub too much will enlarge it to the point that the wheel will chatter, which slows the racer down. This is the same as making the axle too small by over-polishing (this is mentioned in the axle section of this guide).

Less wheel contact is faster.

We found that racers whose wheels had minimal contact with the track were faster than those whose wheels fully contacted the track. Also the wheels should be the *only* contact that the racer has with the track. Other sections of this guide have addressed clearances, and the axle section of this book shows one method of connecting the axles to the body to ensure minimal wheel contact.

WHEEL RECAP

- Make sure that the wheels are round.
- Make sure that the internal hubs of the wheels have no defects and are clean.
- When installing the wheels, make sure that they are properly aligned (all four are parallel) and that there is minimal contact with the track (they should run on the inside edge).

14

Axles

The four nails that act as axles to the wheels of the racers are an important piece of the rolling train. The axles perform two specific functions that we found to be critical. The first is that they hold the wheel in a specific position. We found three specific characteristics critical to speed, wheel alignment, and axle angle.

Racers with aligned wheels are faster.

Wheel alignment is a no-brainer! When we tested this characteristic, we found that racers with good alignment were faster than those without.

Racers with axle angles of five to ten degrees are faster.

Axle angle also plays a role in the speed of the racer. Having the axles angle upward from five to ten degrees has two effects on the racer. First, it minimizes the amount of the wheel surface that contacts the track. Consider this fact; the less wheel surface that contacts the track, the less friction that occurs to slow the racer down. Second, the angle of the axle causes the wheel to move to the outside, pulling it away from the racer's body. This reduced the fiction caused by contact of the wheel hub with the racer body. Whatever angle you chose for one axle, make it consistent for all of the other axles. If you choose ten degrees, make all of the axles ten degrees.

Racers with three wheels touching the track are faster.

The third discovery was made quite by accident. When you are adjusting the axles, lift one of the front axles slightly more than the other three. What you are looking for is to actually pick that wheel slightly off of the running surface. In other words, your racer should only run on three wheels! There is no simpler and faster way to reduce the overall friction of the wheels (in fact this move reduces the friction by 25 percent). Another discovery that we made was to leave the area where the wheel hub touches the car body unpainted. Paint actually slows the wheel. We also burnished the wood in this area by rubbing it with steel wool and graphite. This made the area more slippery. (See Figure 7.)

Racers with prepared axles are faster.

Some of the most interesting discoveries that we made were related to the axles. Much focus is normally placed on polishing and tuning the axles. We found that:

1. Too much polishing of the axles (giving them a mirror-like finish) actually causes more drag and the racer to run slower.

2. Axles that had lateral scratches or lines in them were the fastest.

3. Removing the small gussets increased a racer's speed. (See Figure 8.)

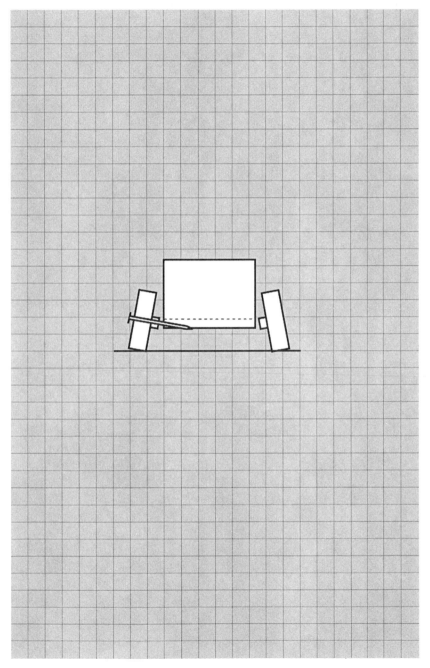

Figure 7

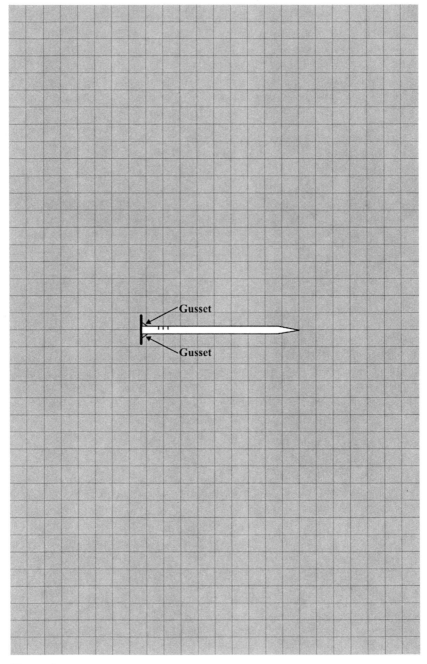

Figure 8

15

Proper Lubrication

The icing on the cake, when it comes to minimizing friction, is proper lubrication. You are limited by the rules to use only powdered graphite or the Cub Scout approved white, Teflon powder.

Through testing, we found little difference between the two lubricants. However, we did find that over a series of races, racers that were *properly* lubricated with graphite powder performed consistently better. The important word is "properly." Lubrication of the wheels is not as simple as sprinkling graphite powder into the space between the axle and the wheel. Lubrication of the surfaces is a multiple-step process. If you prepared the wheels and axles as described in previous sections, then the following steps will help optimize your racer's speed. Please note that graphite can make a mess. Work in an area that contains your lubricant. This also helps you recycle it.

1. Place a wheel (outside up) on a flat piece of cardboard or paper.

2. Pour or sprinkle graphite powder into the hole until it is full.

3. Using a toothpick, a paper clip, or small stick, tap the graphite powder down.

4. Repeat steps one through three until you can no longer tap any graphite into the hole.

5. Repeat steps one through four on the remaining three wheels.

The next steps will push out most of the graphite that you just put in the wheel hub.

1. With the wheel lying as positioned in the previous steps (outside facing upward), push an axle through the center hub. You will only push a short way in before the axle hits the bottom.

2. Repeat this procedure with the remaining wheels and axles.

3. Turn the wheels over, one at a time, while holding their axle in place and pushing it all the way through the hub (the wheels should now be upside down with the point of the axle pointing upward).

4. With the end of a toothpick, force as much graphite powder into the gap between the nail and the hub (you have now created a wheel assembly).

5. Carefully pick up a wheel assembly. (Do not allow the nail to slide in the hub. The flanged end of the axle will hold the graphite in the hub.)

6. Insert the axle into the wheel groove until there is about one-sixteenth of an inch of clearance between the wheel hub and the point that it would make contact with the racer's body.

7. Repeat step six with the three remaining wheels.

Now spin each of the wheels for about five minutes each. Remember that graphite will be flying everywhere! Do not do this over areas that stain!

After you have conditioned the wheel surfaces, remove the wheels and repeat the entire process, up to, but not including, the spinning of the wheels. Now set your racer away in a safe place until race day.

16

The Quick Guide to Building a Fast Racer

There are no shortcuts to building the fastest pinewood derby racer. The following guide and checklist will help you make a fast racer using most of the characteristics detailed in the previous chapters of this book. If your time is limited and you only can follow this guide, it is better than just cutting into the wood, sanding it somewhat smooth, painting it, and hammering the axles into place.

Step 1. Draw out your design to actual size. On a piece of heavy paper or light cardboard, such as a manila file folder, draw out your racer. The best way to ensure that you are working within the exact dimensions is to place the block of wood, provided in the kit, on the paper and trace around it.

It is recommended that you first trace the side view. Do not forget to mark the location of the axle grooves. Then turn the block on its top or bottom, and trace it again. This rectangle will be your top view. Then place the block on end, and again trace this twice. These two rectangles will be your front and rear views. This is what you should have when you are finished with Step 1. (See Figure 9.)

Step 2. Draw your design limits on the rectangles. These limits are those characteristics that PCR identified as significant to improving your racer's speed. These limits include wheel hub relief in the body of the racer (to reduce friction), horizontal nose relief (to minimize the chance of the front of the racer bottoming out), and nose taper (to aid in track alignment). When you are complete with Step 2, your drawing should look like this. (See Figure 10.)

Step 3. You are now free to design your racer, as long as you stay within the limits. When you are complete with this step, your template should look something like this. (See Figure 11.)

Step 4. Cut out the shapes you created, and with a pencil or marker, use them as guides to transfer the design to the block of wood. Do not throw the templates or stencils away. You can use them later to check the racer's symmetry.

Step 5. Rough cut the shape you want. "Rough cut" means that you should cut on the outside of your lines.

Step 6. Sand and smooth your racer's shape. Use the templates to check for right- and left-sided symmetry. That means check to make sure that both sides of the racer are the same.

Step 7. Once the body is the shape that you want, weigh all of the components (the body, four wheels, and four axles). Add weights to bring it within one-eighth ounce of five ounces (a minimum four and seven-eighths ounces).

Step 8. Prime and paint the racer's body. When it is dry, weigh it again, and adjust the weights to bring it to five ounces or slightly less.

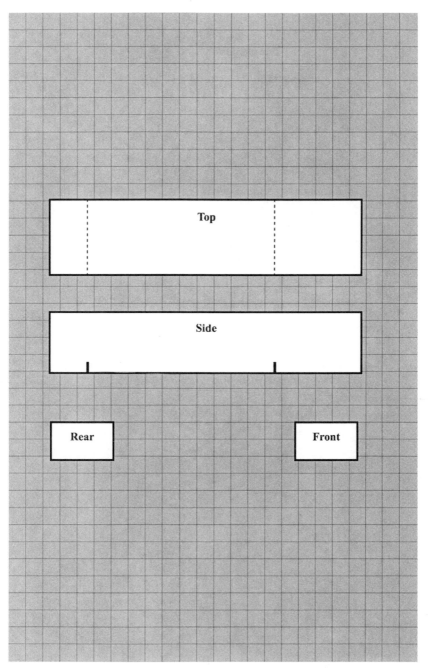

Figure 9

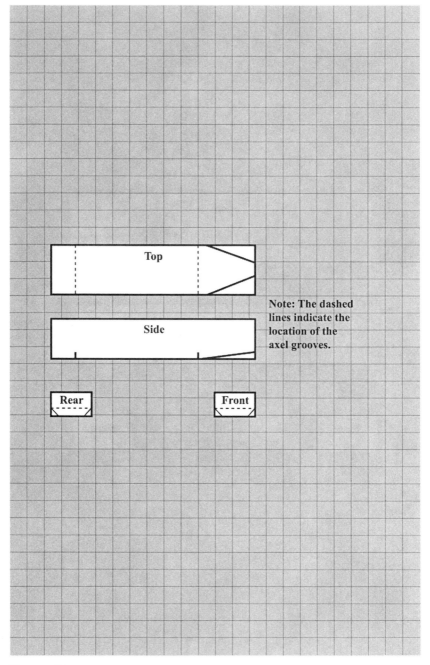

Note: The dashed lines indicate the location of the axel grooves.

Figure 10

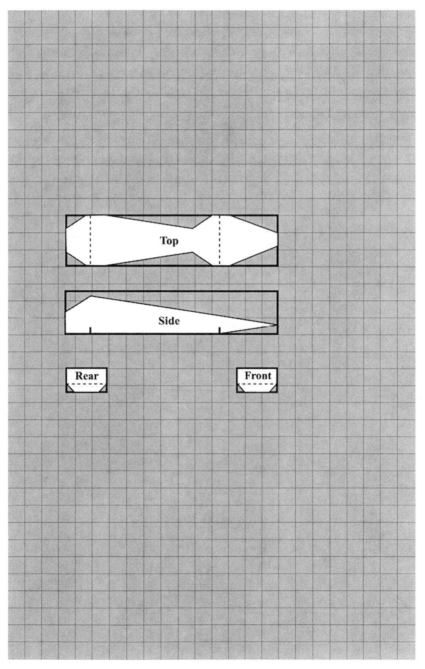

Figure 11

Step 9. Install the wheels and axles. Only three of the four wheels should be touching the ground. All of the axles should angle slightly upward, approximately five degrees. Weigh the racer one more time to ensure that it doesn't go over five ounces. Also test the racer to see if it runs in a straight line on a flat surface. If it doesn't, push the axle in the proper direction, as if you were steering it.

Step 10. Lubricate the wheels by carefully pouring graphite in the gap between the wheel and the axle. Spin each wheel a few times and repeat until you are satisfied that a sufficient amount is in this space.

You are now ready to race!

Good luck!

17

Closing Thoughts and Suggestions

Almost everyone is tempted to do things to their racers to obtain an edge in the race. It is simple as going out on the Internet and ordering machined wheels, special lubricants, and/or polished and relieved axles, or just buying a pre-built car. Scouting is an organization that promotes honesty, honor, integrity, pride, fair play, and sportsmanship, to name a few. Chances are that the pre-race inspectors are simply volunteer dads or moms. They are not aware of all of the various ways that a person can cheat in a race as simple as the pinewood derby. Most cheaters will get away with it. Do not teach your son this lesson. Cheating in the pinewood derby is a seed that can grow into other actions like blood doping, steroids, or even another Enron! The two simplest and most important lessons to be learned through the pinewood derby are "doing your best" and "winning by the rules."

Just when you thought you knew everything there is to know!

During the course of writing this book, we came upon a breakthrough concept! We hurriedly tested the hypothesis and found that the performance of the racer was the best ever experienced! In fact, it consistently ran under two seconds. That is two-tenths of a second faster than the best time we previously recorded! Since this discovery is unique, we are seeking a ruling from the BSA. If we find that it is within the rules, we'll disclose it to you on our website.

SHARING YOUR DISCOVERIES

We realize that we have probably not thought of or tested everything possible. If you find a characteristic that makes a difference, and it is within the rules, please go to our website *www.PinnacleCarRacing.com* and share it with other builders. The pinewood derby will be more exciting for your contribution.

Good luck from Pinnacle Car Racing!

There is nothing better than winning by the rules!